Raising a RED FLAG

An Analysis of
The One Project

Jan Voerman

TEACH Services, Inc.
P U B L I S H I N G
www.TEACHServices.com • (800) 367-1844

Copyright © 2014 TEACH Services, Inc.
ISBN-13: 978-1-4796-0426-5 (Paperback)
ISBN-13: 978-1-4796-0427-2 (ePub)
ISBN-13: 978-1-4796-0428-9 (Mobi)
Library of Congress Control Number: 2014956183

Published by

TEACH Services, Inc.
P U B L I S H I N G
www.TEACHServices.com • (800) 367-1844

Table of Contents

Introduction

We are living in dangerous times. The end is near and the powers of darkness are overactive, knowing that time is short. Satan's aim is to seduce the elect and destroy those who have built their faith on the truth. That is why, when we see danger approaching our fellow brothers and sisters in Christ, we are to blow the trumpet and sound the alarm.

The Bible calls us to be alert and awake as the end draws near. Just before the coming of Christ, when the ten virgins are all asleep, wake up calls are urgently needed in order that as many as possible may be saved in God's coming kingdom.

> *Just before the coming of Christ, when the ten virgins are all asleep, wake up calls are urgently needed in order that as many as possible may be saved in God's coming kingdom.*

Love and brotherly unity of all people is the heralded watchword of the popular movements in our day. Although love and unity are necessary in the Christian life, these important aspects should never eclipse God's righteousness. A true movement of God will be characterized by restoring the principles of God's broken law among humanity. This is the only way that will bring true love, happiness, unity, and salvation.

On the surface the popular movements of our day look attractive, beneficial, and innocent, but when put to the test by God's standard, I am concerned that underneath lurks unholy principles that exert unnoticed, baneful influences.

There should be in our midst no room for doubtful movements and activities. Our intentions may be pure and sincere, but we must be careful not to identify with movements that are not thoroughly sound and in harmony with God's purpose.

Within this book I will examine two unrelated movements that simply share the same name—The One Project—and the same concept of transformation. One is a project which includes secular aspects and implications and promotes shared global values and New Age concepts; the other is run by Adventists and promotes focusing solely on Jesus. By studying these two movements, one in the world and one in the church, I hope to stimulate discussion and cause us to analyze the messages that fight for our attention and call us to change our thinking.

The One Project:

A Secular Viewpoint

Stephen Ridley, a fellow of the Royal Society of Arts and a Chartered Certified Accountant, holds a master's degree in technology management and is founder of The One Project. He lives in England and has written two books: *The Book of Life* and *The Book of Intention.* Both books play a key role in promoting his message and the philosophy behind The One Project, a philosophy that is clearly oriented in New Age thinking.

The Book of Intention reveals a pantheistic idea, for we read on page 3: "God is the good in all." On the same page, the question is raised, "Do I believe in God?" to which he responds, "No, I do not believe in God, but I *know* that God exists. I have both surrender and faith."

One page earlier, Ridley wrote, "The One Project ... is about the Universe. It intends a better world for all Human Beings based on love. *The Book of Intention* expands upon *The Book of Life*, explaining the nature of reality, why we are here, and how to grow to a higher level of consciousness, towards a higher self, both as practical Human Beings and through the spirituality and connection that is innate within everyone. This work is both a channeled and experiential understanding of holistic philosophy, psychology, healing and prophecy, uniting the work of the avatars and their messages, a Book of *knowledge*. It is about learning, healing and teaching, intending to unite all Human Beings as One."

The reference to the work of *avatars* and their messages unmistakably reveals the link with the New Age movement as promoted by New Age priestess Alice Bailey in her books.

According to The One Project's website, the project features the sharing of global values and the transformation of human consciousness for the Golden Age. There are three aspects in this sentence that catch our attention:

- Sharing global values

- Transformation of human consciousness

- Preparation for the Golden Age

Does the gospel of Jesus Christ call us to share global values, or are we as Christians to share the truths of the Bible? It is true that our human consciousness should be influenced and transformed according to God's will, but this expression is meant here as a *human change* of thinking as a preparation for the Golden Age. Does the Bible really say that a Golden Age for humanity on earth will soon be here? It is clear that these three aspects do not match biblical teaching. No, they clearly match New Age thinking.

Alice Bailey, New Age priestess, contemplative, mystic, and occultist, coined the term New Age, and she revealed the often unnoticed operations behind the scenes. Note how she pictures the transformation of human consciousness or changed thinking:

It is this growing spirit of humanitarianism which will lie behind all movements towards world socialisation in the various nations. This movement is symptomatic of a change in the orientation of man's thinking, and therein lies its major value…. it is at the same time foundational to the new world order which will emerge out of all these experiments which human thinking is at this time evolving. These are the things which will be in the consciousness of disciples commissioned by the Hierarchy to bring about the needed changes and the new orientation. (Bailey, *The Externalisation of the Hierarchy*, p. 584)

The idea is to bring about the transformation of human consciousness with new schools of thought:

Together and as a group they can become sensitive to the incoming new ideas which it is intended should condition the new age that is upon us; *together and as a group* they can establish the ideals and develop the techniques and methods of the new schools of thought which will determine the new culture; together and as a group they can bring these ideas and ideals into the consciousness of the masses, so that schools of thought and world religions can be blended into one, and the new civilization can emerge. (Ibid., pp. 29, 30).

This, however, is not God's program for mankind, and it is not in harmony with His plan of redemption. This world will not be saved by human effort of changed thinking but only by faith in our crucified and risen Saviour. He alone is able to change our thinking so that we focus on heavenly things and the ways of the Holy Spirit.

A New World by Human Effort

The vision of The One Project is to create and live in a world guided by *shared global values*, benefiting all and One.

This will create a new beginning for Humanity, manifested by thinking and acting through the shared values of

Collaboration, Constructiveness and *Benevolence*. This in turn creates a virtuous circle in everything Human Beings do, leading to the *transformation of Human consciousness*.

Development of a new global economic model that maintains a sustainable environment will also ensure the survival of Human Beings on Earth, ultimately creating a world on that is fit for future generations.

The other pages on The-One-Project.net website give recommended reading and inspirational resources for personal learning, the transformation of Human consciousness, *and on collaborative, constructive and benevolent* projects *already taking place. ("The One Project-Home Page," The One Project, http://1ref.us/6n)*

As we consider this information, it should be clear that The One Project seeks to create a new world by human effort—"a new global economic model"—that will ensure the survival of mankind on earth for future generations. The vision is to create and live in a world guided by shared global values.

As Christians we should lovingly care for each other and for the earth as good stewards, but is the creation of a better world by human effort the digest of biblical teaching? Is that the world we should be looking for as Christians? Is that the message we should proclaim? No, we should be proclaiming the good news that God will create a new heaven and earth. Human efforts are doomed to fail. The One Project harmonizes with the principles of the New World Order and with New Age thinking.

Note that the intended transformation of human consciousness is not by the influence and work of the Holy Spirit but by thinking and acting through the shared values of collaboration, constructiveness, and benevolence.

Under the "Recommended Reading" link we find five books, including *The Power of Now: A Guide to Spiritual Enlightenment* by Eckhart Tolle. A description of this book is as follows: "Surrender to the present moment, where problems do not exist. It is here we find our joy, are able to embrace our true selves and discover that we are already complete and perfect. If we are able to be fully present and take each step in the Now we will be opening ourselves to the transforming experience of THE POWER OF NOW. It's a book to be revisited again and again."

In this book we are again squarely confronted with New Age thinking. Note, for instance, that the book presents the idea that we are already complete and perfect. Thus man's divinity is affirmed. This is in harmony with the New Age statement in *The Externalisation of the Hierarchy*: "Step by step man has been led through prayer, the voice of desire, through worship, the recognition of deity, through affirmation of the fact of human identity of nature with the divine, to a belief in the divinity of man" (p. 400). How misleading and unbiblical! Yet, The One Project promotes this thinking by suggesting that individuals interested in the movement read these other books.

Another one of the five recommended books to read is: *Quantum Healing: Exploring the Frontiers of Mind/Body Medicine* by Dr. Deepak Chopra. The description of this book is as follows:

This is an extraordinary new approach to healing by an extraordinary physician-writer - a book filled with the mystery, wonder, and hope of people who have experienced seemingly miraculous recoveries from cancer and other serious illnesses. Dr Deepak Chopra, a respected New England endocrinologist, began his search for answers when he saw patients in his own practice who completely recovered after being given only a few months to live. In the mid-1980s he returned to his native India to study Ayurveda, humanity's most ancient healing tradition.

Now he has brought together the current research of Western medicine, neuroscience, and physics with the insights of Ayurvedic theory to show that the human body is controlled by a 'network of intelligence' grounded in quantum reality. Not a superficial psychological state, this intelligence lies deep enough to change the basic patterns that design our physiology - with the potential to defeat cancer, heart disease, and even aging itself. In this inspiring and pioneering work, Dr Chopra offers us both a fascinating intellectual journey and a deeply moving chronicle of hope and healing.

Who is Dr. Deepak Chopra? He is an Indian medical doctor and writer who specializes in mind-body medicine. Chopra says he has been influenced by the Vedanta philosophy. He was initiated in the Transcendental Meditation movement, which he later left because of its "cultish atmosphere." He practices Ayurvedic medicine, a traditional Hindu form of medicine. He is the founder and director of the holistic Chopra Center for Wellbeing in Carlsbad, California ("Deepak Chopra," Wikipedia, http://1ref.us/6o).

From this brief explanation of the book and Dr. Chopra's credentials, it should be clear that the book presents ideas that are not consistent with God's principles of healing. No, the book has more to do with the spirit world and the powers of darkness than God. We can be sure that satanic agencies are at work with increasing activity as we near the end of time.

> *We can be sure that satanic agencies are at work with increasing activity as we near the end of time.*

Ellen White cautioned that we must guard ourselves against wonderful healings that will take place in Satan's name: "Wonderful scenes, with which Satan will be closely connected, will soon take place. God's Word declares that Satan will work miracles. He will make people sick, and then will suddenly remove from them his satanic power. They will then be regarded as healed. These works of apparent healing will bring Seventh-day Adventists to the test" (White, *Last Day Events*, pp. 166, 167).

Working Together

In addition to New Age ideas that promote human effort and alternative medicine, The One Project advocates a new global economic model in which we do away with greed and corruption. That is a noble idea that has roots in biblical principles. However, should the church interfere with business and the economy? The One Project takes its cue from New Age thinking that promotes everyone being as "one."

> The common people are today awakening to the importance and responsibility of government; it is therefore realised by the Hierarchy that before the cycle of true democracy ... can come into being, the education of the masses in cooperative statesmanship, in economic stabilisation through right sharing, and in clean, political interplay is imperatively necessary. The long divorce between religion and politics must be ended, and this can now come about because of the high level of the human *mass* intelligence. (Bailey, *The Externalisation of the Hierarchy*, pp. 479, 480).

The influential pastor Rick Warren of the Saddleback Church testified that he had trained around 400,000 pastors in 162 countries along with countless business and government leaders, thus joining church and state as The One Project suggests. Says Rick Warren: "But now, my staff and I are not just training church leaders but business and government leaders and help them too.... A three-legged stool will have stability. So, I'm going from country to country teaching business its role, teaching church its role, and teaching government leaders their role—you've got to work together" (Voerman, *The Hidden Agenda*, p. 116). But shouldn't there be a separation between church and state?

Warren made a clear link with the economic world when he trained churches and states to work together. His universal "purpose driven PEACE plan" should usher in the much desired millennium—the Golden Age or a new and better world. Under the influence of New Age thinking, I believe that there is a clear bearing between Warren's teaching and the principles of The One Project. This could explain, to some extent, that the ideas of The One Project—shared resources, collaboration with others, elimination of greed—have been embraced by several evangelical churches .

It is also important to note that the modern evangelical church growth movements advocate a similar transformation of consciousness called "a paradigm shift"—a change of mind from the old to the new way of thinking—derived from Peter Drucker, a prominent expert in business management: "It is no accident that the church-growth leaders present this globalistic 'paradigm shift' of thinking, that is in harmony with Drucker's methodology and with the New Age Movement, as a central spearhead on the way to the One World Church" (Voerman, *The Hidden Agenda,* p. 85). Thus there is a link between many evangelical churches, business, and the New Age movement.

Love and Brotherhood

All of the modern movements emphasize to a great extent the importance and values of love and brotherhood as a main issue. The One Project does the same and has the word love in bold and italic letters on their website under the heading "Shared Global Values" in an effort to emphasis its importance. We read: "The key to the transformation of Human Consciousness, the second coming, is the manifestation of shared values across the world, across all cultures, faiths and belief systems of the common good, the values of *love*" (*"The One Project-Shared Global Values," The One Project, http://1ref.us/6p*).

Note also the emphasis on love and brotherhood by the New Age movement: "The work of pouring out the principle of love (which is the Christ principle) and of lifting the masses in their consciousness to the pitch where they can understand and welcome that love-principle is the main work of the new age, and it will inaugurate the age of brotherhood and mould humanity into the likeness of the Christ" (Bailey, *The Externalisation of the Hierarchy*, p. 504). "The Christ" in this quotation is not Jesus Christ of the Bible but the New Age Cosmic Christ whose coming will be esoteric. "'Cosmic Christ' does not refer to Jesus, but to Satan himself, the great anti-Christ who will mimic Christ's return" (Voerman, *The Hidden Agenda,* p. 174).

Consider the reason why the cosmic Christ has not yet come and the Golden Age has not yet been ushered in:

> The reason He has not come again is that the needed work has not been done by His followers in all countries. His coming is largely dependent, as we shall later see, upon the establishing of right human relations. This the church has hindered down the centuries, and has not helped because of its fanatical zeal to make "Christians" of all peoples and not followers of the Christ. It has emphasised theological doctrine, and not love and loving understanding as Christ exemplified it. The Church has preached the fiery Saul of Tarsus and not the gentle Carpenter of Galilee. And so, He has waited. (Bailey, *The Reappearance of the Christ,* p. 12).

Note that there are two things that delay the second coming of the cosmic Christ and the ushering in of the New Age:

- The establishment of right human relations.

- The lack of emphasis on love and loving understanding.

It is very interesting to note that these two things are the main points of The One Project, which clearly include right human relations on the basis of shared values of love: "The key to the transformation of Human Consciousness, the second coming, is the manifestation of shared values across the world, across all cultures, faiths and belief systems of the common good, the values of *love*."

Thus we see again that there is harmony with the New Age movement and The One Project, as is further articulated by the

following quote, which stresses the importance of love: "An Ava-
tor is at present usually a Representative of the second divine aspect, that of Love-Wisdom, the Love of God…. Humanity needs
love, understanding and right human relations as an expression of
attained divinity" (Bailey, *The Reappearance of the Christ,* p. 11).
Consider the New Age activity and influence on the churches:
"The activity of the astral plane is being much intensified and the
angels of devotion, in whom the aspect of divine love is pre-em-
inent, work with the astral bodies of all those who are ready to
strengthen and redirect their spiritual aspiration and desire. They
are the angels who guard the sanctuaries of all the churches, cathe-
drals, temples and mosques of the world. They are now increasing
the momentum of their vibration for the raising of the consciousness of the attendant congregations" (Bailey, *The Externalisation
of the Hierarchy,* p. 505).

Ellen White wrote in harmony with this: "An innumerable host
of evil angels are spreading over the whole land and crowding the
churches" (White, *Early Writings,* p. 274; compare with Rev. 18:2).

The Adventist One Project

Five Adventist church leaders—Alex Bryan, Japhet De Oliveira, Sam Leonor, Tim Gillespie, and Terry Swenson—founded The One Project, a movement within the church with the mission of focusing solely on Jesus. This, certainly, is a good theme. To walk with Jesus, have a good relationship with Him, get to know Him better, and serve Him in a more efficient way are all, without doubt, good and desirable aspects of the project.

However, I feel that it is important to evaluate the project and ask some questions so as to make sure we are on sure footing. Has, in a sense, the Adventist version of The One Project something to do with the existing One Project movement outside our church? Are there perhaps some similar aims and purposes? Does the Adventist version, for instance, also promote a change of thinking or, in other words, a transformation of human consciousness? Does it somehow reflect New Age thinking? Does it advocate global unity by sharing love rather than doctrine? These are certainly important questions that I seek to answer based on my personal observations and analysis of the project.

The Seattle Gathering

On February 10 and 11, 2014, The One Project hosted a gathering in Seattle under the title *Jesus. All: Present Truth*.

Janet Lundeen Neumann was invited to attend the event. Afterwards, she wrote an article for ADvindicate. Within the article, she noted that there was continued live rock music during the two days of the conference, and her impression was that the notion of *change* was overtly urged—no defined change, simply change.

> I continued listening for an Adventist version of "Present Truth," but instead heard a revised truth—a nebulous truth that focused on "conversation" and "dialogue," with consensus determining direction. I heard people disillusioned with the established church structure, some seeking to deconstruct traditional worship. I heard an urging that a "narrative" truth be interpreted by "current culture." I heard an advocacy for a social gospel with no mention of evangelism. I heard an urgency that we dip into "other streams" and "streams that flow both ways" for truth. And I heard mockery of our church both in word and in tone from the platform and attendees. I heard an emergent truth. (Neumann, "One Project: Present or Emergent Truth?" ADvindicate, http://1ref.us/6q)

In his welcome speech, cofounder Japhet De Oliviera stated that "nothing is etched in stone"; "It's OK to turn around 180 degrees"; "The more we know the more uncertain we become" (Ibid.). In response to these statements, Neumann wrote in her article, "He merely sowed the verbal seeds of uncertainty and indefinite change" (Ibid.).

Speaker, Bill Knott, emphasized *conversation* and *dialogue*, by making the following statements: "Disagreement is important to our growth"; "Jesus expects disagreement in His church" (Ibid.). Yet, I would remind him that Christ prayed for His disciples that they would be unified in their mission to reach others for Him (John 17). And weren't the members of the early church unified (Acts 2:46; 4:32)?

Another cofounder, Alex Bryan, told a story of a young woman he had recently met who had become paranoid after attending a Revelation Seminar by an Adventist evangelist. Bryan urged that we, as a church, should not go around scaring people, frightening them with fearful images of beasts. Instead of scaring people, he suggested that the church should focus on Jesus.

We find one of the most startling and misleading statements of The One Project in their official publication *For the One: Voices from the One Project*: "He [Jesus] Himself was and is the message, not His teachings" (Brown, p. 23). But what else could His teachings be? Ellen White says, "People from all nations listened to his teaching, and carried the message to all parts of the world." ("Words of Comfort—No. 2," *The Review and Herald*, October 26, 1897). We can be sure that the teachings of Christ are the only true life-giving message to save mankind.

My concern is that if we somehow disregard the things Jesus taught we present only *part* of Jesus. We even reject Him if we belittle or neglect the prophecies revealed in the book of Revelation, for it is the "Revelation of Jesus Christ" (Rev. 1:1). We can only speak of "Jesus. All." if we give full credit to *all* His teachings, including the words of prophecy He revealed in the book of Revelation.

However, this speaker seemed to dismiss the necessity of sharing the last day message for fear of making people paranoid. Janet remarks: "Present Truth as revealed by Ellen White states, 'The book of Revelation must be opened to the people... The truth it contains must be proclaimed, that people may have an opportunity to prepare for the events which are soon to transpire.' Letter 87, 1896. (Ev. 195.4)" (Neumann, "One Project: Present or Emergent Truth?" ADvindicate, http://1ref.us/6q).

> *We can only speak of "Jesus. All." if we give full credit to all His teachings, including the words of prophecy He revealed in the book of Revelation.*

Randy Roberts, pastor of the Loma Linda University Church, also spoke. He quoted John 16:12 and stressed that today "there is more." He explained that "God moves us forward as we are able." Neumann felt that he was suggesting that there is "new truth" for us to learn in our generation. At the end of his speech, the following message was displayed on the video screens: *"Recalibrate*: When we learn new things, how do we set aside old understandings without damaging our 'roots'?" (Ibid.).

I took it to mean that we should be prepared to learn new things and set aside old understandings. But what does he mean by old understandings? The things we have always believed? The prophecies and doctrines of the Bible that our church is founded on? It is not specified, but undoubtedly, learning new things and setting aside old understandings indicates a change of mind. And is this not, in other words, a transformation of human consciousness?

Sam Leonor, another cofounder of The One Project, seems to take a similar approach to prophecy. At the beginning of his presentation, he showed a picture of a prophetic time table from Daniel and Revelation that was used by our early Adventist pioneers. He then commented that he would "absolutely not" be spending time speaking about the prophecy as our church has done in the past because we are living in "the now." Can we preach "Jesus. All." without focusing on prophecy? For isn't Jesus the fulfillment of prophecy?

Consider this significant quote:

> We are to dwell in our doctrinal discourses upon the truth as it is in Jesus. Present the truth for this time as an important message, from another world. Lift Him up, the Man of Calvary. Come in consecration to holier ground, and still holier. Preach the truth with the power of God sent down from heaven....

> The present truth, the special message given to our world, even the third angel's message, comprehends a vast field, containing heavenly treasures. No one can be excusable

who says, "I will no longer have anything to do with these special messages; I will preach Christ." No one can preach Christ, and present the truth as it is in Jesus, unless he presents the truths that are to

> *"No one can be excusable who says, 'I will no longer have anything to do with these special messages; I will preach Christ.'"*

come before the people at the present time, when such important developments are taking place. (White, *The Voice in Speech and Song,* pp. 325, 326).

Sam Leonor stressed the here and now and stated that "in heaven there is no sickness." Immediately after making that statement, he emphasized that "this should be here now." He went on to say, "In heaven there is no poverty—and that's the way it should be here now." He also said, "In heaven there will be gender equality—and that's what we should work towards here now" (Leonor, "Jesus Is Our Future," One Project, http://1ref.us/79).

This type of language sounds very similar to the message in Eckhart Tolle's book *The Power of Now.* It also sounds like *kingdom now* theology, which comes close to New Age thinking with the Golden Age believed to be just around the corner.

Sam Leonor seems to regard our connection with the prophetic Advent movement rather lightly. He wrote in the official One Project publication: "He [Christ] didn't – and doesn't – call people to follow a religion, a denomination, a congregation, a preacher, a cause or a movement. He calls them to Himself" (Brown, *For the One: Voices from The One Project,* p. 20). Did Christ not intend to call people to be part of His cause, movement, or church?

Note Ellen White's words: "Another obligation, too often lightly regarded,—one that to the youth awakened to the claims of Christ needs to be made plain,—is the obligation of church relationship. Very close and sacred is the relation between Christ and His church,—He the bridegroom, and the church the bride; He the head, and the church the body. Connection with Christ, then, involves connection with His church" (*Education*, p. 268).

Ellen White explicitly says, "In calling His people together in church capacity, God designs that they shall form one Christian family and daily be fitting for membership in the family above" (*In Heavenly Places*, p. 283).

Sam Leonor presents a rather inadequate picture of Christ and His church. It certainly is not a perfect presentation of Jesus. All. It belittles Christ as the head and bridegroom of His church, while the importance and uniqueness of God's end-time Advent cause and movement is eclipsed.

Terry Swenson, another One Project founder, seems to cherish a similar view about the church. He wrote: "If people want to march around saying 'We are the church!' then that's OK. But I'm a follower of Jesus" (*For the One, Voices from the One Project*, p. 151).

I understand that Swenson, in other words, is saying here: When people say, we are the church, OK, that's their idea; but I would not say that, no, I am a follower of Jesus. He clearly stresses that he follows Jesus, as if that is something else as being His church. But is there really a marked difference? Swenson does not seem to realize that being the church and following Jesus is inseparably connected with each other. Says Ellen White: "Christ and His church are inseparable" (*Testimonies*, vol. 3, p. 418). Thus, as noticed before, Connection with Christ involves connection with His church. Ellen White explains: "...in a life of service to Christ, connection with the church is one of the first steps" (*Education*, pp. 268, 269).

Note that the church existed from the beginning, right after the fall: "God had a church when Adam and Eve and Abel accepted and hailed with joy the good news that Jesus was their Redeemer. These realized as fully then as we realize now the promise of the presence of God in their midst" (*The Upward Look*, p. 228). Thus we see that the church is made up of believers who accept Christ as their Redeemer. As Adam, Eve and Abel gladly accepted Jesus, they could truly testify that they formed the church and so there is nothing wrong when faithful believers in Christ confess: *We are the church.*

We should not in any way belittle God's church. "Any betrayal of the church is treachery to Him who has bought mankind with the blood of His only-begotten Son. From the beginning, faithful souls have constituted the church on earth" (*Acts of the Apostles*, p. 11). Thus it is clear that following Jesus means to be part of His church. We do not present Jesus. All, if we focus only on Him and not on His church and teachings.

Cofounder Tim Gillespie shared a story of an imaginary cow that was fed and grew up in a box and never saw anything beyond its box. He stressed that we must go beyond our own denomination. "To remain fresh we must be fed from many streams" through dialogue with others outside the church. He suggested that we could learn and bring about change by engaging with other people outside our walls (Gillespie, "The Way of Jesus," One Project, http://1ref.us/7d).

"To remain fresh we must be fed from other streams—streams must flow both ways—others should inform our present truth. We must dialogue with others. You know why? Because God is always doing something new, and we wouldn't want to miss it. As a church we have always been engaged with one another—we have shut our boundaries tight. We should change; we should learn from others" (Ibid.).

His comments raise some questions in my mind, such as, Has God entrusted us with a special message to share with others or are others to share a special message with us? Are there other streams and truths out there that we are unaware of?

> *Has God entrusted us with a special message to share with others or are others to share a special message with us?*

The Bible says that God's people "did all eat the same spiritual meat; And did all drink the same spiritual drink" (1 Cor. 10:3, 4). Is it possible to preserve the unity for which

Christ so earnestly prayed in John 17 if we all eat and drink from different sources?

I wonder why Gillespie encourages people to be fed from other streams. Are we, in his mind, perhaps destitute of solid truth that we should learn from others? It is interesting to note that in The One Project publication he tells us that he was sitting on a panel while the attention was focused on a discussion of "the settled truth" and consider what he said: "Excuse me, but I have no idea what you mean by 'settled truth' … Yeah, that's not Adventist. Actually that's the most un-Adventist phrase I've ever heard" (Brown, *For the One: Voices from the One Project*, p. 17). Are we to understand from these words that Adventists believe in unsettled truth? As we go on, we may discover new aspects of truth, but that does not unsettle truth, instead it settles it more firmly. Ellen White affirms: "It is as certain that we have the truth as that God lives" (*Testimonies for the Church*, vol. 4, p. 595).

We should realize that our faith is firmly settled. Says Ellen White: "Many of our people do not realize how firmly the foundation of our faith has been laid" (*Selected Messages*, book 1, p. 206). She admonishes us: "We are to hold to the sure pillars of our faith. The principles of truth that God has revealed to us are our only true foundation. They have made us what we are. The lapse of time has not lessened their value. It is the constant effort of the enemy to remove these truths from their setting, and to put in their place spurious theories. He will bring in everything that he possibly can to carry out his deceptive designs" (Ibid., p. 201). It is Satan's purpose to sow doubt, cause discord, and take away the security of our faith. Uncertain, unsettled truth is an end-time characteristic. Ellen White explained: "Nothing stands out in clear and distinct lines, upon rock bottom. This is one of the marked signs of the last days" (Ibid., p. 15).

The various speakers made good points in the messages they presented; however, their comments often raised questions as to the overall direction they are proposing that the church needs to take. To view their presentations and determine for yourself the truth in their messages, you can visit the media section of their website under the "Resources" heading (http://1ref.us/6r).

Education Molds One's Thinking

Preaching the love of Jesus and focusing on His character traits is not the problem. The problem is in some of the other messages that are presented. It is slight and almost undetectable at times, but after listening to many of the cofounders' sermons, I feel that there is an undertone of New Age thinking and the philosophy of the emerging church.

It is interesting to note that many of the cofounders of The One Project have studied at or obtained a degree from George Fox University, a school that promotes the emerging church, contemplative prayer, and spiritual formation. Although we may think we are immune to ideas that are unbiblical, when presented day after day, they creep into our minds and change our philosophies.

Following is a brief outline of the philosophies that George Fox University promotes:

- **Contemplative Spirituality**: "A belief system that uses ancient mystical practices to induce altered states of consciousness (the silence) and is rooted in mysticism and the occult but often wrapped in Christian terminology. The premise of contemplative spirituality is pantheistic (God is all) and panentheistic (God is in all). Common terms used for this movement are 'spiritual formation,' 'the silence,' 'the stillness,' 'ancient-wisdom,' 'spiritual disciplines,' and many others" ("Brennan Manning and Contemplative Prayer," Lighthouse Trails Research, http://1ref.us/6s).

- **Spiritual Formation**: "A movement that has provided a platform and a channel through which contemplative prayer is entering the church. Find spiritual formation being used, and in nearly every case you will find contemplative spirituality. In fact, contemplative spirituality is the heartbeat of the spiritual formation movement" (Ibid.).

- **The Emerging Church:** This movement has many aspects. "The common denominator being promoted is the idea that the time has come for Christianity to be reinvented for our generation. In order to do so, the church must provide the environment and the experiences to attract people. Christianity, the Emerging Church promoters say, must become relevant to our postmodern generation. No longer does reason or God's Word hold the answers to life's questions. Experience must become the key factor to encounter spiritual reality" (Oakland, "The Emerging Church: Another Road to Rome," Understand the Times, http://1ref.us/6t).

Consider the following insight and notice how deeply George Fox University is involved in contemplative spirituality and mysticism: "In addition, George Fox University is a hub of contemplative /emerging activity with a list of adjunct professors that includes Dan Kimball and Leonard Sweet. In 2005, George Fox hired Todd Hunter, Leonard Sweet and Brian McLaren to teach certain classes, and chapel speakers at the university have included Richard Foster and Brennan Manning. Recommended and required reading for classes at George Fox include a wide assortment of staunch contemplatives/mystics like Thomas Keating, Henry Nouwen, and Thomas Merton" ("Conference Alert: Missional Matrix," Lighthouse Trails Research, http://1ref.us/6u)

Richard Foster, one of the speakers at George Fox, has been called a "contemplative spark plug." "More than any other individual, Richard Foster has spread Roman Catholic and Pagan mysticism throughout Protestant and Baptist churches" ("Evangelicals Turning to Roman Catholic Contemplative Spirituality," Way of Life Literature, Inc., http://1ref.us/6v) As an example of its focus, George Fox University offers a course titled "Spirituality and the Writings of the Mystics – Included in the course is a small group practicum to assimilate contemplative practices into the student's devotional life" ("Reader Finds 'An Afternoon With a Spiritual Formation Professor at a North American Bible School' to be 'Junk,'" Lighthouse Trails Research, http://1ref.us/6w).

Its proponents taut that the contemplative prayer, or the spiritual formation movement, is a good way to come closer to God. But is it?

Ray Yungen justly appeals: "I challenge the Christian community to look to the facts surrounding the contemplative prayer movement and see its connection to the New Age occultism and Eastern mysticism... After taking an honest look at the evidence, the conclusion is overwhelming that contemplative prayer is not a spiritually-sound practice for Christians" (*A Time of Departing*, 2nd ed., p. 89, 130; Cf., Voerman, *The Hidden Agenda*, p. 132).

> "'Contemplative Spirituality' also known as the 'Spiritual Formation Movement' smoothly paves the way for the working of evil spirits within the church and in people's lives. The spirits 'will confess faith' and 'respect' church-institutions and 'their work will be accepted as a manifestation of divine power'" (Voerman, *The Hidden Agenda*, 2nd ed., p. 195, 196; Cf., White, *The Great Controversy*, p. 588).

This type of spirituality is evident in some of the messages that the cofounders of The One Project are sharing with their audiences. For example, Sam Leonor presented the message "Good Gifts" at the Forest Lake Church as part of the GODencounters Conference in 2005. At the end of his talk, Leonor referenced the "ancient practice of meditating on the word," saying, "Let these words wash through your soul" (Leonor, "Good Gifts," Vimeo, http://1ref.us/7b). He then slowly read the paraphrased version of the Lord's Prayer with the mystical phrase, "as above, so below" from *The Message* Bible.

Another appropriate title for "The Message," could be The New Age "Bible."

There is so much New Age thought permeating "The Mess," you couldn't learn the Truth from it, no matter how hard you tried.

One piercing example of New Age doctrine occurs right in the middle of the Lord's Prayer. Containing metaphysical connotation, the phrase, "as above, so below", is one of the most recognized in New Age philosophy. This motto is said to hold the key to all mysteries. In fact, all magical systems are believed to function as a result of this formula … One particular book written and published by the editors of the New Age Journal was actually entitled, *As Above, So Below*. Its introduction said, "Thousands of years ago in ancient Egypt, the great master alchemist Hermes Trismegistus, believed to be a contemporary of the Hebrew prophet Abraham, proclaimed this fundamental truth about the universe: As above, so below.' This maxim implies that the transcendent God beyond the physical universe and the immanent God within ourselves are one. Heaven and Earth, spirit and matter, the invisible and visible worlds form a unity to which we are intimately linked." (Swaggart, "The Message Bible: Continued," Francis & Friends, http://1ref.us/7c)

If one has been a student at George Fox University, which promotes New Age spirituality, should we be surprised if he or she reflects and promotes these ideas and practices? It is always a delicate matter to share concerns. As with most controversial subjects, there are usually two groups: one in favor and one against. There are quite a few people in the Adventist Church who do not find fault in the emerging church movement. They dismiss the worries of those who discern the dangers of practicing this kind of spirituality as unwarranted.

However, there are others who are concerned about the emerging church and its ideas, which are infiltrating the Adventist Church because some pastors and leaders are educated by institutions and attend conferences that espouse these beliefs.

The following points speak to the philosophy of one of the founders of The One Project. The purpose of sharing these points is not to personally harm anyone, for the concerns are not particularly against any one person. Instead, the following section is presented in an effort to highlight the philosophies that have emerged because of the education of The One Project presenters.

What follows are concerns that came to light when Alex Bryan's name was proposed as a candidate for the presidency at Walla Walla University. A number of people stepped forward and shared their thoughts about his philosophy.

> As a group of constituents, alumni, educators, pastors, church members, medical professionals, students and parents, we feel that Alex Bryan, at this point in time, is not a good candidate for the next WWU president as evidenced by the concerns expressed in this document.
>
> Out of multiple areas of concern, three follow as to why Alex Bryan, at this point in time, should not be appointed as WWU's next president: 1) his background, 2) his educational experience, and 3) *his views and relationships with spiritual formation*.
>
> 1) Alex Bryan's Background
>
>   a.   Created a "Sunday service" church ... [which] described itself in 2004, while Alex Bryan was the pastor ... [as] "an independent, interdenominational, evangelical church....
>
>   b.   Professional degree in emergent church spiritual formation. Received his Doctor of Ministry degree

from George Fox University, under the direction of the spiritualist and Emerging Church leader Leonard Sweet.

c. Invited his mentor, a self-admitted spiritualist and leader of the emerging church movement, Leonard Sweet, to Southern Adventist University, to speak for Vespers Jan '09 and attempted to indoctrinate the Southern University Theology faculty by bringing Sweet to speak with them specifically.

   [The university released a nine-point statement denouncing the emerging church movement and reaffirming Seventh-day Adventist faith and practice (http://1ref.us/6y)]

d. Opening his pulpit (April 2012, both services) at Walla Walla University Church to emerging church leader Shane Claiborne, a proponent of the "Kingdom Now" theology embraced by the emerging church movement and a teacher of universalism, and founder of the New Monasticism movement. Claiborne's staff admitted one of their objectives, while at WWU, was to recruit WWU students to join them in the work of their ministry.

e. Alex Bryan has called Ellen G. White a 19th century mystic. He has stated this from the pulpit and included references to this in his book, page 22, "In 1842, during this era of Advent hope, fifteen-year-old Ellen White had a mystical experience."

f. Openly promoted Roman Catholic Mystics and Contemplative authors at the Adventist Forum on Spiritual Formation, October 2011. These authors included: Richard Foster, Dallas Willard, Brennan Manning, and Henri Nouwen...

g. During his sermons he often quotes from leading emergent church leaders, such as Leonard Sweet and Catholic contemplative authors
such as Brennan Manning, and many more.
Note that these authors are also listed as "My Fa-
vorites" on his brother's blog, the current pastor of
the Sunday church Alex helped to start. Also, these
authors and their books are listed on Alex Bryan's
blog as "Must Reads." [He quoted, for instance,
from the New Age minded Eugene Peterson in his
sermon "Why I Love the Body," on March 8, 2014;
and N. T. Wright, who teaches a redefined, other
gospel, in his sermon "A Whole New Politics," on
January 7, 2012.]

h. Belittling Adventist doctrines in favor of mystical experiences during his One project sermon February
2012, Seattle Wa. He suggested that our fixation on
doctrine and identity as Seventh-day Adventists has
kept us from becoming a great religion....

His failure to properly shepherd his misguided Roswell,
Georgia flock is disappointing. Former Seventh-day Adventists today are worshiping in the [Sunday] church he
started, now led by his brother...

Bryan continues to promote Spiritual Formation in his
church....

3) Views and Relationship with Spiritual Formation

a. Introduction of Spiritual Formation. Alex Bryan has
indicated that Spiritual Formation shall be incorpo-
rated in all venues of the WWU church.

b. ...

c. Ecumenical Focus

i.   Some constituents were at the One Project gathering February, 2011. Bryan presented a bowl with puzzle pieces that he used to demonstrate that the SDA church, even as we are unique; we are only one of the pieces of the puzzle.

[Note this comment from someone who watched a video of Bryan speaking at the Seattle One Project meeting: "WHAT?? So he's saying that we don't have a unique identity and purpose. That we aren't God's last day church. We're just one of many churches that God has spread his truths over. So there's no difference if I leave the SDA church and become a catholic then?" ("Seattle SDA Identity and Purpose," YouTube, http://1ref.us/7f)]

ii. He speaks often of the need to be ecumenical. This emphasized joining with other denominations and leaving behind our Adventist distinctiveness and practice. For example, at the ONE project, Bryan stated that if a Seventh-day Adventist called themselves part of the "remnant church" then they are "arrogant and extremists."

d. Doctrinal Concerns

i.   Seventh-day Adventist beliefs are rarely presented from the pulpit. The Three Angels' Messages, the Sanctuary message, the Remnant, the distinctive messages of Adventism are not being heard....

Alex Bryan displays his favorite Spiritual Formation books at the Adventist Forum meeting held at Walla Walla University, October 2011....

Bryan recommends reading Contemplative Pastor Eugene Peterson, Emerging Church leader Brian Mclaren's Generous Orthodoxy, and Universalist Rob Bell's Velvet Elvis. ("Concerns Over Alex Bryan Email Posted for the Curious," Adventist Media Response and Conversation, http://1ref.us/6x, emphasis added)

Some may try to dismiss these points as only "rumors," but on the other hand, others, including seminary students, are concerned about the teaching and philosophy of Alex Bryan as is noted in a letter written by Lois Kind and posted on Mike's Bible Study Yahoo group. She wrote,

"We are a group of Seventh-day Adventist church members in the Walla Walla Valley deeply concerned with what is sweeping into our Walla Walla University and valley churches. We do not wish to remain a silent majority....

In July Pastor Alex Bryan introduced the new Associate Pastor, Emily M. Flottmann, who will be leading out in 'Spiritual Formation'. In his sermon that day he used the words 'Spiritual Formation, mysticism, mystical,' etc. At one time during the July sermon, he referred to Ellen G. White as a mystic and suggested that we should be reading from outside sources. We are very concerned about the way these ideas will be presented to impressionable college students, as well as to younger children in their formative years. Parents send their children here in good faith and pay thousands of dollars so that they will be instructed in the truth. What will be their anguish when they discover these students have been indoctrinated in spiritual sophistries?...

Pastor Bryan defended the use of Richard J. Foster's books knowing full well that Foster is a Quaker mystic, the head of Renovare, an organization whose goal is to introduce evangelicals to contemplative spirituality. Foster borrowed many of the principles in his book, Celebration of Discipline: The Path to Spiritual Growth from the Desert Fathers (mystics in Egypt of the third and fourth centuries) and from Ignatius Loyola's Spiritual Exercises. Pastor Bryan produced a pile of books, including some by Brennan Manning, a former Catholic priest, which he recommended for the spiritual journey."

You can read the entire letter by visiting: http://1ref.us/6z.

Mysticism

On May 24, 2014, the Walla Walla University community experienced a unique church service, which you can view on their church website. Alex Bryan preached about prayer, and he requested that all the lights be turned off during his sermon. In complete darkness he repeated many times: "Close your eyes when you pray." He further explained that "in the darkness you shall see even more clearly." He stressed the value of darkness as a necessity to communicate with God, since Jesus prayed to God at night. He also appeared to be inspired by a fourteenth century English monk who wrote *The Cloud of Unknowing*, which he quoted from, as follows:

> This darkness and cloud is always between you and God, no means what you do, and it prevents you from seeing him clearly by the light of your reason and from experiencing him in sweetness of love in your affection. So set yourself to rest in this darkness as long as you can, always crying out after him whom you love. For if you are to experience him or to see him at all, insofar as it is possible here, it must always be in this cloud and in this darkness.

"So set yourself to rest in this darkness as long as you can … if you are to experience him or to see him … it must always be in this cloud and in this darkness." Truth and error were mixed into this sermon on prayer. Where did his ideas on prayer come from? Was it by chance from his education? Although Jesus prayed at night when it was dark, isn't darkness linked with evil powers? Are Christians not children of light, called out of darkness? Do we not serve God who is only light and in whom is no darkness at all? Why then should we sit in darkness as we pray and worship Him?

I find it interesting that the leaders of the emerging church also talk about darkness as a good thing. Dan Kimball, who studied with Alex Bryan at George Fox University under Leonard Sweet, wrote *The Emerging Church,* and in it he explains: "But in our culture, which is becoming more multi-sensory and less respectful of God, we have a responsibility to pay attention to the design of the space where we assemble regularly. In the emerging culture, darkness represents spirituality. We see this in Buddhist temples, as well as Catholic and Orthodox churches. Darkness communicates that something serious is happening" (Kimball, *The Emerging Church*, p. 136).

> *Do we not serve God who is only light and in whom is no darkness at all? Why then should we sit in darkness as we pray and worship Him?*

However, does darkness not represent *false* spirituality? Is it not symbolically used to portray ignorance, falsehood, and wickedness? And is darkness not particularly associated with demonic activities and occult practices?

The emerging church leaders are convinced that Christianity needs to be adjusted and revised in order to meet the spiritual needs of this new, modern age. This is in full harmony with the teaching of the well-known priest and New Age leader Matthew Fox who promotes mysticism and contemplative prayer. Fox wrote:

> In addition to welcoming silence, a cosmological worship will welcome darkness as well, and in the process instruct people to embrace the dark and not fight it. Of course we cannot read in the dark and since so many worshipers in

the West have learned to equate prayer with reading, the idea of turning out the lights may threaten many people. Yet prayer is mostly about responding with the heart, not with the written word. Worship that takes the heart as the starting point for prayer would be sure to attract many who have given up on worship precisely because it has banished mystery and darkness... It is time to place worship within the cosmological setting that the human species through-out the world is embracing. We should explore the rituals of the native peoples, whose ceremonies appreciated the power of darkness and night. (*The Coming of the Cosmic Christ*, pp. 220, 221)

The following quote provides further insight into the quote that Bryan included in his sermon that focused on a cloud of dark-ness. Evelyn Underhill, a pacifist and mystic, wrote the introduc-tion for *The Cloud of Unknowing*, describing the book as written for "lovers of mysticism." She explained, "It represents the first expression in our own tongue of that great mystic tradition of the Christian Neoplatonists which gathered up, remade, and 'salted with Christ's salt' all that was best in the spiritual wisdom of the ancient world" (*The Cloud of the Unknowing*, p. 2).

There is no particular information about the author of *The Cloud of Unknowing*, but it seems clear that he was a cloistered monk, possibly a Carthusian, devoted to the contemplative life. This mystical source is treasured by Catholics.

Carl McColman, contemplative author, speaker and retreat leader - *Embrace Silence - Embody Love* - writes:

Anonymously written around the year 1375, *The Cloud of Unknowing* — a lucid and deceptively simple manual on contemplative spirituality — offers a fascinating glimpse into the practical side of medieval mysticism ... The Cloud's author advocates contemplation: prayer steeped not in language or the imagination, but in cultivated inner silence ... One remarkable feature of *The Cloud of Unknowing* is that it advocates the use of a single-syllable 'prayer word' to effectively discipline the mind and to keep it focused while the heart attempts to grow in its supramental task of loving God. This spiritual exercise involves repeating a short word like 'God' or 'love' repeatedly, in order to help surrender all extraneous thoughts and seek the place of inner silence, where one may 'be still and know' the God who is lavish love. This practice of using a prayer word has been adapted in our own day by the monks who developed the method of centering prayer, a form of meditation which again relies on the repeated single-syllable word as a tool of 'centering' or allowing the mind and body to come to a place of resting in the Divine presence ... In the eyes of God, we are already mystics and contemplatives. All we have to do, now, is to learn how to simply allow that to unfold. Even within the mysterious mists of the cloud of unknowing. (http://1ref.us/7a)

The Cloud of Unknowing is advertised as "the glory of English mysticism, and one of the most practical and useful guides to finding union with God ever written" ("The Cloud of Unknowing," bol.com, http://1ref.us/70). An experience "of union with God ... is not a Christian concept, but rather, a Pantheistic principle" (Dominick, *Outcome-Based Religion: Purpose, Apostasy, & The New Paradigm Church*, p. 301; Cf., Voerman, *The Hidden Agenda*, p. 146).

    The Cloud of Unknowing is not an innocent source that we as Christians should read and quote from in church—it is without doubt a dangerous source.

    Ray Yungen, author, speaker, and research analyst, referring to *The Cloud of Unknowing*, explains: "It is essentially a manual on contemplative prayer ... The premise ... is that in order to really know God, mysticism must be practiced—the mind has to be shut down or turned off so that the cloud of unknowing where the presence of God awaits can be experienced.... even though the method is identical to occult and Eastern practices... By definition, a mystic ... is someone who uses rote methods in an attempt to tap into their inner divinity. Those who use these methods put themselves into a trance state outside of God's sanction or protection and thus engage in an extremely dangerous approach" (Yungen, *A Time of Departing*, 2nd ed., pp. 33, 34).

Contemplative Spirituality is "a belief system that uses ancient mystical practices to induce altered states of consciousness (the silence) and is often wrapped in Christian terminology; the premise of contemplative spirituality is pantheistic (God is all) and panentheistic (God is in all)" ("Contemplative Prayer," Lighthouse Trails Research, http://1ref.us/71).

Thus, the spiritual practice advocated in *The Cloud of Unknowing,* to repeat a word over and over again (Cf., Matt. 6:7) and to silence the mind in order to unify with God, is an occult, New Age practice of emptying the mind and realizing the divinity within.

Contemplative spirituality "plays a very important role in the New Age movement. As attractively wrapped in biblical terms, it subtly entices and wins Christians to occult concepts and practices" (Voerman, *The Hidden Agenda,* p. 128).

"Always the tools of contemplative prayer are used only to help guide us to an experience of union with God. In the temporal moment of contemplative prayer we are drawn even momentarily into the eternal realm that transcends our time" ("Contemplative Prayers," Presbyterian Mission Agency, http://1ref.us/72). "'Into the eternal realm that transcends our time' is a new age expression. And the method advocated is designed to induce a form a self-hypnosis, which removes reason and will and prepares one to become the subject of 'wicked spirits in high places'" (Voerman, *The Hidden Agenda*, p. 145).

Brian Flynn, a former New Age medium, explains: "It is unbridled and unprotected mental thought that provides a perfect avenue for a demonic spirit world to intercept and redirect our way of thinking" (Flynn, *Running Against the Wind,* p. 93).

The mystical practices advocated in *The Cloud of Unknowing* are dangerous for Christians to dabble with. Therefore, it is unwarranted to cite this source in a church worship service.

Knowing that the education of the founders of The One Project is steeped in New Age contemplative spirituality and mysticism, one questions what messages they have ingested in their studies are being regurgitated in their presentations and sermons. After listening to them speak, I observed belittling of Adventist doctrine in favor of mystical experiences. They mingle biblical principles with unholy ideas and practices.

We are warned: "More harm can be done by one who has a mixture of truth and error, than many who teach the whole truth can undo and correct" (White, "Be of One Mind," *The Review and Herald*, May 29, 1888).

It is also interesting to note that on a forum website about The One Project, some people clearly recognize the dangerous influence of the emergent church ("The One Project," RevivalSermons.org, http://1ref.us/73).

Guest Speaker

Leonard Sweet appeared as a special guest speaker at the 2014 Seattle One Project gathering. He is a well-known influential author who teaches New Age ideas and mystic spirituality, pantheism and panentheism. He promotes ecumenism and the emerging church. In his book *Quantum Spirituality*, he admires prominent New Age leaders such as Willis Harman, Matthew Fox, and M. Scott Peck. He even calls them "extraordinary" and "great" New Light Leaders and characterizes them as his "personal role models and heroes of the true nature of the postmodern apologetic" (p. viii. Cf., Warren Smith, *A "Wonderful" Deception,* pp. 106, 107).

In one of Sweet's other books, *Soul Tsunami,* he stresses the urgent need to accept the new concepts. "It is time for a 'Postmodern Reformation' and everybody must choose: 'Reinvent yourself for the 21st century or die'" (Sweet, *Soul Tsunami,* p. 75, as quoted in Voerman, *The Hidden Agenda*, p. 161).

So why was Sweet invited to speak at the Seattle gathering? With the educational background of The One Project founders, it was apparently no problem at all to have this New Age promoter of the emergent church as a special guest speaker. Although he may have presented a good message, he still promotes New Age thinking, and yet he was still invited to speak at a meeting of Adventists. Does this fact have any meaning at all? Could it be indicative of the direction The One Project is headed? All five founders of The One Project have an established connection with Leonard Sweet, which was evident at the 2012 Seattle gathering in which the attendance fee included a copy of Sweet's book *I am a Follower: The Way, Truth, and Life of Following Jesus.* With this background information in mind, which direction is The One Project movement headed and what is it really promoting?

Change Your Church

As the 2014 Seattle gathering neared its end, a communion service was held in which participants shared bread and juice and engaged in a kind of anointing service instead of foot washing. Everyone anointed the hand of the one sitting to the right with a drop of oil, while a blessing was read from a card: "May you be blessed with compassion for those around you, the courage to be who you are, gentleness and a tender heart, openness, understanding, and respect, strength that shines from within, and the power to make Jesus. All" (Neumann, "One Project: Present or Emergent Truth?" ADvindicate, http://1ref.us/6q).

Janet Lundeen Neumann was not happy with the wording of this blessing. She wrote, "When I expressed a discomfort with the line that asks for 'strength that shines from within,' and changed it to 'strength that comes from God,' I was quickly admonished by a person sitting near me that 'I know these people and they're not into that kind of stuff.' Even so, the 'strength that shines from within' belief is panentheistic" (Ibid.).

As for the anointing ceremony, such practices are one of the characteristics of the emerging church, which is meant to comply with the idea that post-moderns are looking for a more sensual experiential worship. The sacred signs of water, bread and juice, oil and laying on of hands are accentuated. Julie B. Sevig, editor and author, explains: "Post-moderns prefer to encounter Christ by using all their senses. That's part of the appeal of classical liturgical or contemplative worship: the incense and candles, making the sign of the cross, the taste and smell of the bread and wine, touching icons and being anointed with oil" (Sevig, *The Lutheran*, "Ancient New," Sept., 2001, as quoted by Oakland, "The Emergence of the Eucharist in the Emerging Church," Understand the Times, http://1ref.us/74).

The title of The One Project—Jesus. All.—holds much promise, but does it meet the expectations of those who are seeking a deeper relationship with Jesus based solidly on the Bible?

Of course, there are many who feel that The One Project hits the mark; however, there were also disappointed attendees. Neumann remarks, "As the event drew to a close, a 'charge' was given to each of us. Not a charge to share Jesus, but a charge for 'change.' Each person was told to 'go home and change your church'… There was no focus on a continuing walk with Jesus by emulating His life, changing our lives, modifying our lifestyles, or sharing the Present Truth in the context of the three angel's messages. It was just 'Jesus. All.' That's all! Without any biblical or concise definition" (Neumann, "One Project: Present or Emergent Truth?" ADvindicate, http://1ref.us/6q).

Pastor Chad Stuart concludes: "In summary I would say, it was not the gathering I expected, but this does not mean it was a bad gathering. The focal point I expected, learning more about Jesus and drawing nearer to Jesus, was not the primary focus I experienced, and based on that alone I would probably not choose to attend again" ("The One Project Analysis," Outside the Pulpit, http://1ref.us/75).

On Friday evening, October 24, 2014, Janet Neumann from the Walla Walla area spoke at the Sacramento Central Seventh-day Adventist Church. The title of her presentation was "Omega Emerging: A Church in Change," and she presented aspects of the emerging church movement, spiritual formation, and The One Project. Her presentation can be viewed on YouTube: http://1ref.us/7g.

Another presentation of interest was given by Pastor Steve Wohlberg at Southern Adventist University. Titled "Perils of the Emerging Church," the presentation includes valuable information about The One Project and can also be viewed on YouTube: http://1ref.us/7h.

The dangers of the emerging church, mysticism and spiritual formation, and The One Project were also addressed at a symposium and can be viewed and listened to on the Operation Iceberg website: http://1ref.us/7k. Besides a few speeches dealing particularly with The One Project, the Town Hall Panel video provides some very interesting information about The One Project.

Conclusion:

The Emerging Church

As we come to the close of this short examination of The One Project—both the secular and Adventist missions—it should be clear that some of the messages are aligned with New Age thinking and false, mystic spirituality, which is practiced in the emerging church movement. This movement is strongly ecumenical and does not characterize the uniqueness of Christianity but pictures it as one voice among many. Dialogue and spiritual practices are the way to experience God, while the Bible is not regarded as the sole source for faith and practice. Ideas and spiritual practices are also adopted from multiple religious sources, including Catholicism, Islam, Buddhism, and Eastern mysticism.

Within the Adventist Church, there are others who are concerned about the emerging church movement and its philosophies. The faculty of Southern Adventist University released a nine-point statement on October 23, 2013 in an effort to reaffirm Adventist beliefs (http://1ref.us/76). I urge you to read the document for yourself.

Some may object to a study like this because it reveals negative aspects about our church or because it feels like an attack on other brothers and sisters in Christ. However, if we do not analyze what others are saying against the Bible, even within our church, we open ourselves up to be deceived and led astray.

> *If we do not analyze what others are saying against the Bible, even within our church, we open ourselves up to be deceived and led astray.*

You may argue that there are also many good things about The One Project. Of course there are attractive things in almost all movements, but the point is that it should not be *partly* good. Are all points of The One Project good and truthful and biblical? There are many different churches out there, and they all have some good, biblical points, but God wants His church to be truthful and holy in *all* aspects. He is not satisfied with less. His aim is "a glorious church, not having spot, or wrinkle, or any such thing; but that it should be holy and without blemish" (Eph. 5:27).

Do we really need to be counseled and influenced by people outside our church who promote the modern emerging church movement with mystical, spiritual formation practices? Should such people be our teachers in order to be better educated and equipped to fulfill our God-given mission? Has God left His church destitute of important aspects of spirituality and truth? Is it God's purpose that we should go and learn truths and practices from teachers outside our church who neglect His law and do not keep holy His sign of their sanctification? Should we invite them as our special guest speakers to educate us? Is that the way Christ leads His church now in this time of the end? Is that the way in which we can have a closer walk with Jesus and be prepared and ready for His soon coming?

We are assured that we are not destitute of truth. "God has given all these truths to His children who are being prepared for the day of God.... If God has any new light to communicate, He will let His chosen and beloved understand it, without their going to have their minds enlightened by hearing those who are in darkness and error" (White, *Early Writings*, p. 124).

It does not matter how great, brilliant, important, and popular other teachers may be; if they are not in full harmony with God's law, they should not be our counselors. "There is to be no compromise with those who make void the law of God. It is not safe to rely upon them as counselors. Our testimony is not to be less decided now than formerly; our real position is not to be cloaked in order to please the world's great men. They may desire us to unite with them and accept their plans, and may make propositions in regard to our course of action which may give the enemy an advantage over us" (White, *Selected Messages*, book 2, p. 371).

Dedicated workers who are well trained and sufficiently educated can be, without doubt, a great blessing in God's work. However, sometimes there is a desire to obtain a degree from a seminary or university outside of our church without fully realizing the involved consequences of such a move. Even if it is a well-known reputable Christian institution, there will be differences of opinion that will certainly influence our thinking. It is never good to expose ourselves to teachings that may endanger and challenge our religious persuasion.

Note this important counsel: "We need men well trained, well educated, to work in the interests of the churches. They should present the fact that we cannot trust our youth to go to seminaries and colleges established by other denominations; that we must gather them into schools where their religious training shall not be neglected…. If we do not have schools for our youth, they will attend other seminaries and colleges, and will be exposed to infidel sentiments" (White, *Counsels to Parents, Teachers, and Students*, p. 45).

The One Project's strong emphasis to go beyond our own denomination to be fed from other streams is not in harmony with God's inspired counsel. We are admonished: "Do not now make mistakes. Never, never seek to remove one landmark that the

Lord has given His people. The truth stands firmly established on the eternal Rock—a foundation that storm and tempest can never move…. Do not lower the banner of truth or allow it to drop from your hands in order to unite with the solemn message for these last days anything that will tend to hide the peculiar features of our faith" (White, *Testimonies for the Church,* vol. 8, p. 162).

The emerging church brushes biblical doctrine and prophecy aside. Philip Yancey, author and editor for *Christianity Today,* whose beliefs fit with emerging spirituality, wrote: "Perhaps our day calls for a new kind of ecumenical movement: not of doctrine, nor even of religious unity, but one that builds on what Jews, Christians, and Muslims hold in common" (Yancey, "Hope for Abraham's Sons," *Christianity Today,* November, 1, 2004).

The influential pastor Rick Warren, a great supporter of the emerging church movement, showed a very low regard for Bible prophecy; he "was actually laying ground work for the emerging church's new reformation, a reformation that rejects thinking about the return of Christ and works more at convincing the multitudes that Christ is already in them as a global christ-consciousness" (Oakland, "Rick Warren Says Those Who Focus on Bible Prophecy 'Not Fit for the Kingdom of God,'" Lighthouse Trails Research, http://1ref.us/77).

Warren dismissed the sure word of prophecy clearly. He wrote: "When the disciples wanted to talk about prophecy, Jesus quickly switched the conversation to evanglism. He wanted them to concentrate on their mission in the world. He said in essence, 'The details of my return are none of your business. What is your business is the mission I've given you. Focus on that!... focus on fulfilling your mission, not figuring out prophecy'" (Warren, *The Purpose Driven Life,* p. 285).

Warren actively discourages the study of the prophetic word because he considers this a snare of Satan to keep us from our mission. We are warned however: "Satan is not asleep; he is wide awake to make of no effect the sure word of prophecy. With skill and deceptive power he is working to counterwork the expressed will of God, made plain in His word" (White, *Testimonies for the Church*, vol. 9, p. 92).

"Every day adds its sorrowful evidence that faith in the sure word of prophecy is decreasing, and that in its stead superstition and satanic witchery are captivating the minds of many" (White, *Prophets and Kings,* p. 210; Cf., Voerman, *The Hidden Agenda,* pp. 59–63).

Sources from outside our church may be very interesting to read and when the author is known to be a dedicated Christian who faithfully lives up to the light he has received, it may even be a blessing to read his works. However, it makes a great difference if the author is influenced by New Age ideas and by mystical, ancient spiritual practices. In such cases it would be strongly advisable to shun such unholy sources, regardless of how popular and brilliant the author and his works may appear to be. We should never allow such people in any way to be our guides, teachers, educators, and counselors.

If we are called as God's people and led by Him, as "the special object of His care and of His love" (White, MR 168, 169), should we go to other denominations and be fed from their streams and be educated, guided, and counseled by their sources, even when unholy links are obvious? If we do so, would we not be like Israel of old who "committed two evils; they have forsaken me [God] the fountain of living waters, and hewed them out cisterns, broken cisterns, that can hold no water" (Jer. 2:13)? And are we not just as Israel of old, confronted with that significant question: "And now what hast thou to do in the way of Egypt, to drink the waters of Sihor? Or what hast thou to do in the way of Assyria, to drink the waters of the river?"(verse 18).

Consider God's impressive response: "Thine own wickedness shall correct thee, and thy backslidings shall reprove thee: know therefore and see that *it is* an evil *thing* and bitter, that thou hast forsaken the LORD thy God, and that my fear *is* not in thee, saith the Lord God of hosts" (verse 19).

Is it advisable to drink and be fed from streams and sources from other denominations which are in conflict with the Creator of heaven and earth? Can we be sure then that they have the right spirit or are they perhaps guided by another spirit? Note this very significant statement: "God has a controversy with the churches of today.... They have divorced themselves from God by refusing to receive His sign. They have not the spirit of God's true commandment-keeping people" (White, *S.D.A. Bible Commentary*, vol. 7, p. 979).

Thus it is clear that there is a remarkable difference between God's people who keep His commandments and other churches. We are not just another piece of the puzzle like any other piece, as Alex Bryan, one of the One Project founders, would have us to believe.

Bryan does not seem to see a great difference between other churches and the Advent movement. He even wrote, "The Advent movement was born in failure rather than success, error rather than truth, darkness rather than light, and sorrow rather than joy. Jesus didn't return" (Brown, *For the One: Voices from the One Project*, p. 26).

Was the Advent movement really born in failure, error, darkness, and sorrow? These are strong words that do not demonstrate much esteem for our Adventist heritage. It is true that Christ didn't return as was expected, but did that make the Advent movement an erroneous failure?

Alex Bryan does not appear to recognize God's hand in the Advent movement as did Ellen White. She testified: "But God had led His people in the great advent movement; His power and glory had attended the work, and He would not permit it to end in darkness and disappointment, to be reproached as a false and fanatical excitement. He would not leave His word involved in doubt and uncertainty" (*The Great Controversy*, p. 410).

The Advent movement, instead of being born in failure, error, darkness and sorrow, was a glorious manifestation of God's prophetic timeline. Ellen White wrote, "The advent movement of 1840–44 was a glorious manifestation of the power of God; the first angel's message was carried to every missionary station in the world, and in some countries there was the greatest religious interest which has been witnessed in any land since the Reformation of the sixteenth century" (Ibid., p. 611).

Instead of focusing on the fact that Adventism was a result of God's leading, Bryan repeats: "The stream of Adventism is fed by the teardrops of the Great Disappointment" (*For the One: Voices from the One Project*, pp. 26, 30). Bryan seems not to realize that even in the disappointment of the early Advent believers God's guiding hand was present and that it was by His providence that their faith was tested and grew. Ellen White explains: "Those who were obedient to the message stood out free and united. A holy light shone upon them. They renounced the world, sacrificed their earthly interests, gave up their earthly treasures, and directed their anxious gaze to heaven, expecting to see their loved Deliverer. A holy light beamed upon their countenances, telling of the peace and joy which reigned within. Jesus bade His angels go and strengthen them, for the hour of their trial drew on. I saw that these waiting ones were not yet tried as they must be" (*Early Writings*, pp. 249, 250). "God led his people in the advent movement, even as he led the children of Israel from Egypt. In the great disappointment their faith was tested as was that of the Hebrews at the Red Sea" (*The Great Controversy*, p. 457).

Bryan continues: "Adventism isn't peculiar or special because of our Sabbath-keeping, vegetarian cuisine, or remnant claims. Adventism's uniqueness is found at its historical root: Jesus" (*For the One: Voices from the One Project*, p. 31).

We should certainly uplift Jesus and love Him dearly. But as we know from Scripture, when we love Him dearly, we will keep His commandments. It makes us special and unique because we keep the Sabbath; thus, as Adventists we are repairing the breach that was made in His law. Doesn't the Bible identify God's remnant people as those who keep God's commandments, including the Sabbath? Loving Jesus and keeping His commandments will certainly place us in a *peculiar* position. Ellen White confirms: "Commandment-keeping Adventists are occupying a peculiar, exalted position" (*The Re-view and Herald*, September 7, 1886). Note also this quotation:

> God's people have a special work to do in repairing the breach that has been made in His law; and the nearer we approach the end, the more urgent this work becomes. All who love God will show that they bear His sign by keeping His commandments. They are the restorers of paths to dwell in ... Thus genuine medical missionary work is bound up inseparably with the keeping of God's commandments, of which the Sabbath is especially mentioned, since it is the great memorial of God's creative work. Its observance is bound up with the work of restoring the moral image of God in man. This is the ministry which God's people are to carry forward at this time. This ministry, rightly performed, will bring rich blessings to the church. (White, *Testimonies for the Church*, vol. 6, pp. 265, 266)

Bryan should, as a faithful leader of God's church, stress the important and special ministry of the Adventist Church for this time, but instead he presents an unbalanced picture that diminishes the special work that God has called His remnant church to perform.

But how is it possible that some other denominations appear to be very spiritual, active, and successful, as if God is particularly blessing them, while our church is struggling with several issues and seems to be spiritually tame? Is this not a good argument to go to them to learn the secret of their prosperity and success? Consider, however, this clear explanation: "Satan deceives some with Spiritualism. He also comes as an angel of light and spreads his influence over the land by means of false reformations. The churches are elated, and consider that God is working marvelously for them, when it is the work of another spirit" (White, *Early Writings*, p. 261).

If the roots of the spiritual practices of a church or any religious body are not directly based upon the Bible, but go back to ancient mysticism, then we can be sure that the reformation we may observe is not from God, but the work of other spirits. However, God has honest children in various churches and religious denominations who will be called out from these bodies and who will gladly receive the truth. "Satan knows this; and before the loud cry of the third angel is given, he raises an excitement in these religious bodies, that those who have rejected the truth may think that God is with them. He hopes to deceive the honest and lead them to think that God is still working for the churches. But the light will shine, and all who are honest will leave the fallen churches, and take their stand with the remnant" (Ibid.).

We need to study the Bible as our only source of guidance and examine the simplicity of Christ's example. We should study and follow the faith of the great cloud of witnesses, which is presented to us in the Bible, and we should learn from their experiences. I encourage you to watch an excellent video that was put together by a number of prominent Seventh-day Adventists who address the issue of spiritual formation (http://1ref.us/78).

In closing, consider Ellen White's words of warning against a false reformation of change that will enter the church:

> The enemy of souls has sought to bring in the supposition that a great reformation was to take place among Seventh-day Adventists, and that this reformation would consist in giving up the doctrines which stand as the pillars of our faith, and engaging in a process of reorganization. Were this reformation to take place, what would result? The principles of truth that God in His wisdom has given to the remnant church, would be discarded. Our religion would be changed. The fundamental principles that have sustained the work for the last fifty years would be accounted as error. A new organization would be established.

Books of a new order would be written. A system of intellectual philosophy would be introduced. The founders of this system would go into the cities, and do a wonderful work. The Sabbath of course, would be lightly regarded, as also the God who created it. Nothing would be allowed to stand in the way of the new movement. The leaders would teach that virtue is better than vice, but God being removed, they would place their dependence on human power, which, without God, is worthless. Their foundation would be built on the sand, and storm and tempest would sweep away the structure.

Who has authority to begin such a movement? We have our Bibles. We have our experience, attested to by the miraculous working of the Holy Spirit. We have a truth that admits of no compromise. Shall we not repudiate everything that is not in harmony with this truth?

I hesitated and delayed about the sending out of that which the Spirit of the Lord impelled me to write. I did not want to be compelled to present the misleading influence of these sophistries. But in the providence of God, the errors that have been coming in *must be met*" (White, *Selected Messages*, book 1, pp. 204, 205).

Note also the words that introduce the book *Meet It: Iceberg of Deception—A Look Beneath the Surface* by Rick Howard: "On the surface it looks promising, but when delving under the superficial outer layers, the powers of darkness are found lurking. At an October 2011 meeting of The One Project group, eleven authors were noted as being 'the most helpful.' Yet, they all promote and support the emerging church, spiritual formation interests. They all endorse and advance mysticism and spiritism, and all of them are leaders and teachers of these principles that are designed to win souls to Romanism."

Satan delights to deceive people with truths wrapped up in lies; he rejoices in misleading people with good, attractive, pleasing things that are mingled with falsehood and unholy principles.

It was Moses who stood in the gate of the camp and confronted the people with an important, searching question: "Who is on the Lord's side?" (Exod. 32:26). What is *your* answer to this decisive question?

May God bless all of us as we seek to stay alert and remain true and faithful to His cause.

Bibliography

Anonymous. *The Cloud of Unknowing.* London: John M.
Watkins, 1922.

Bailey, Alice. *The Externalisation of the Hierarchy.* New York,
London: Lucis Publishing Company, 1957.

———. *The Reappearance of the Christ.* New York, London:
Lucis Publishing Company, 1948.

"Brennan Manning and Contemplative Prayer." Lighthouse
Trails Research. http://1ref.us/6s
(accessed August 28, 2014).

Brown,Nathan; Alex Bryan, Japhet De Oliveira, eds. *For the One:
Voices from the One Project.* Warburton, Victoria, Australia:
Signs Publishing, 2014.

"The Cloud of Unknowing." bol.com. http://1ref.us/70
(accessed August 28, 2014).

"Concerns Over Alex Bryan Email Posted for the Curious."
Adventist Media Response and Conversation.
http://1ref.us/6x (accessed August 28, 2014).

"Conference Alert: Missional Matrix." Lighthouse Trails
    Research. http://1ref.us/6u (accessed August 28, 2014).

"Contemplative Prayer." Lighthouse Trails Research.
    http://1ref.us/71 (accessed August 28, 2014).

"Contemplative Prayers." Presbyterian Mission Agency.
    http://1ref.us/72 (accessed August 28, 2014).

"Deepak Chopra." Wikipedia. http://1ref.us/6o
    (accessed August 27, 2014).

Dominick, Mac. *Outcome-Based Religion: Purpose, Apostasy, &
    The New Paradigm Church.* Cutting Edge Ministries, 2005.

"Evangelicals Turning to Roman Catholic Contemplative
    Spirituality." Way of Life Literature, Inc. http://1ref.us/6v
    (accessed August 28, 2014).

Flynn, Brian. *Running Against the Wind.* 2nd ed. Silverton, OR:
    Lighthous Trails Publishing, 2005.

Fox, Matthew. *The Coming of the Cosmic Christ.*
    San Francisco, CA: Harper & Row Publishers, 1988.

Gillespie, Tim. "The Way of Jesus." One Project. http://1ref.us/7d
    (accessed September 2, 2014).

Howard, Rick. *Meet It: Iceberg of Deception—A Look Beneath the
    Surface.* Coldwater, MI: Remnant Publications, 2014.

Kimball, Dan. *The Emerging Church.* Grand Rapids, MI:
    Zondervan Publishing House, 2009.

Kind, Lois. "Dangers of Being Deceived and Misled by 'Spiritual
    Formation.'" Mike's Bible Study. http://1ref.us/6z (accessed
    November 12, 2014).

Leonor, Sam. "Good Gifts." Vimeo. http://1ref.us/7b
     (accessed September 2, 2014).

———. "Jesus Is Our Future." One Project. http://1ref.us/79
     (accessed September 2, 2014).

Neumann, Janet Lundeen. "Omega Emerging: A Church in
     Change." YouTube. http://1ref.us/7g
     (accessed November 12, 2014).

———. "One Project: Present or Emergent Truth?"
     ADvindicate. http://1ref.us/6q (accessed August 27, 2014).

Oakland, Roger. "The Emergence of the Eucharist in the
     Emerging Church." Understand the Times. http://1ref.us/74
     (accessed August 28, 2014).

———. "The Emerging Church: Another Road to Rome."
     Understand the Times. http://1ref.us/6t
     (accessed August 28, 2014).

———. "Rick Warren Says Those Who Focus on Bible Prophecy
     'Not Fit for the Kingdom of God.'" Lighthouse Trails
     Research. http://1ref.us/77 (accessed September 1, 2014).

"The One Project-Home Page." The One Project.
     http://1ref.us/6n (accessed August 27, 2014).

"The One Project-Shared Global Values." The One Project.
     http://1ref.us/6p (accessed August 27, 2014).

"The One Project." RevivalSermons.org. http://1ref.us/73
     (accessed August 28, 2014).

"Reader Finds 'An Afternoon With a Spiritual Formation
     Professor at a North American Bible School' to be 'Junk.'"
     Lighthouse Trails Research. http://1ref.us/6w
     (accessed August 28, 2014).

Ridley, Stephen. *The Book of Intention.* Balboa Press, 2012.

Stuart, Chad. "The One Project Analysis." Outside the Pulpit. http://1ref.us/75 (accessed August 28, 2014).

Swaggart, Frances. "The Message Bible: Continued." Francis & Friends. http://1ref.us/7c (accessed September 2, 2014).

Sweet, Leonard. *Quantum Spirituality.* Dayton, OH: United Theological Seminary, 1991.

———. *Soul Tsunami.* Grand Rapids, MI: Zondervan Publishing House, 1999.

Tolle, Eckhart. *The Power of Now: A Guide to Spiritual Enlightenment.* Novato, CA: New World Library, 2010.

Voerman, Jan. *The Hidden Agenda.* 2nd ed. Ringgold, GA: TEACH Services, Inc., 2011

Warren, *The Purpose Driven Life.* Grand Rapids, MI: Zondervan Publishing House, 2002.

White, Ellen G. "Be of One Mind." *The Review and Herald,* May 29, 1888.

———. *Counsels to Parents, Teachers, and Students.* Mountain View, CA: Pacific Press Publishing Association, 1913.

———. *Early Writings.* Washington, DC: Review and Herald Publishing Association, 1882.

———. *Education.* Mountain View, CA: Pacific Press Publishing Association, 1903.

———. *The Great Controversy.* Mountain View, CA: Pacific Press Publishing Association, 1911.

———. *In Heavenly Places.* Washington, DC: Review and Herald Publishing Association, 1967.

———. *Last Day Events.* Boise, ID: Pacific Press Publishing Association, 1992.

———. *The SDA Bible Commentary.* Vol. 7. Washington, DC: Review and Herald Publishing Association, 1957.

———. *Selected Messages.* Book 1. Washington, DC: Review and Herald Publishing Association, 1958.

———. *Selected Messages.* Book 2. Washington, DC: Review and Herald Publishing Association, 1958.

———. *Testimonies for the Church.* Vol. 4. Mountain View, CA: Pacific Press Publishing Association, 1881.

———. *Testimonies for the Church.* Vol. 6. Mountain View, CA: Pacific Press Publishing Association, 1901.

———. *Testimonies for the Church.* Vol. 8. Mountain View, CA: Pacific Press Publishing Association, 1904.

———. *Testimonies for the Church.* Vol. 9. Mountain View, CA: Pacific Press Publishing Association, 1909.

———. *The Voice in Speech and Song.* Boise, ID: Pacific Press Publishing Association, 1988.

———. "Words of Comfort—No. 2." *The Review and Herald,* October 26, 1897.

Wohlberg, Steve. "Perils of the Emerging Church." YouTube. http://1ref.us/7h (accessed on November 12, 2014).

Yancey, Philip. "Hope for Abraham's Sons." *Christianity Today,* November, 1, 2004.

Yungen, Ray. *A Time of Departing.* 2nd ed. Silverton, OR: Lighthouse Trails Publishing, 2006.

We invite you to view the complete
selection of titles we publish at:

www.TEACHServices.com

Scan with your mobile device
to go directly to our website.

Please write or email us your praises, reactions, or
thoughts about this or any other book we publish at:

TEACH Services, Inc.
P U B L I S H I N G
www.TEACHServices.com • (800) 367-1844

P.O. Box 954
Ringgold, GA 30736
info@TEACHServices.com

TEACH Services, Inc., titles may be purchased in bulk for
educational, business, fund-raising, or sales promotional use.
For information, please e-mail:

BulkSales@TEACHServices.com

Finally, if you are interested in seeing
your own book in print, please contact us at

publishing@TEACHServices.com

We would be happy to review your manuscript for free.